THE

SCOUNDREL'S DICTIONARY,

OR AN

EXPLANATION

OF THE

CANT WORDS

Used by the *Thieves, House-Breakers,*
Street-Robbers and *Pick-Pockets* about Town.

To which is prefixed,

Some curious DISSERTATIONS on the

ART of WHEEDLING;

And a Collection of their FLASH SONGS,
with a proper GLOSSARY

The Whole printed from a Copy taken on one of their Gang, in the late Scu-
file, between the Watchmen and a Party of them on Clerkenwell-Green;
which Copy is now in the Custody of one of the Constables of that Parish

═══════════════════════

LONDON
Spradabach Publishing
2023

SPRADABACH PUBLISHING
BM Box Spradabach
London WC1N 3XX

*The Scoundrel's Dictionary, or an Explanation
of the Cant Words Used by the Thieves, House-Breakers,
Street-Robbers and Pick-Pockets about Town. To Which
is Prefixed, Some Curious Dissertations on the Art
of Wheedling; and a Collection of Their Flash Songs,
with a Proper Glossary. The Whole Printed from
a Copy Taken on One of Their Gang, in the Late Scuffle
between the Watchmen and a Party of Them
on Clerkenwell-Green; Which Copy is Now in the
Custody of One of the Constables of That Parish*

First published in 1754

First Spradabach edition published 2023
© Spradabach Publishing 2023

Interior design by Alex Kurtagic

ISBN 978-1-909606-41-8

British Library Cataloguing-in-Publication Data:
A catalogue record for this book is available from the British Library.

Table of Contents

Note on This Edition

he text in the present volume is based on the 1754 edition published in London for J. Brownnell. It is reproduced here in its entirety.

The spelling and punctuation have been left as in the original, and so has the capitalisation, except in compound terms, where both the constituting words have been capitalised, as opposed to only the initial word. The italicisation has been equally left as in the original, except where an entire block of quoted verse was italicised; in those instances the text has been rendered in Roman type. Obvious typographical errors have been silently corrected.

The Introduction

Since Wheedling and Canting may be justly termed Brethren, I don't think it any ways amiss to joyn them together; not for the Desire I have that any should learn them, in order to Practice; but rather, that knowing them, and to what Wickedness they tend, all that love their own Repose, may shun and avoid the evil Courses they tend to. Nor is Ignorance the least Cause why so many plunge themselves into Wickedness; for, could Sin be truly discovered in its Deformity, it would look so monstrous that the Terrors of its Visage would affright those that court it, from its foul Embraces; nor is it less observable, that those who are least skilled in the Nature of Poisons, are frequently destroyed by Intoxication, especially where it is in their Power to meet unwittingly with the mortal Bane: The Devil too gilds over his Allurements and Temptations with a seeming Good, on Purpose that the Ignorant may take them for what they really are not, and so, unadvisedly, infect their Souls; from which, we may conclude, that to know the Failures and Vices of others, as they are really so, and properly delivered in their proper Shapes and Defects, is the proper Way to grow in Hatred with them, and to avoid them: And therefore, to leave, however, those without Excuse, that read this Part of my Book, I proceed to treat of *Wheedlers*, *Canters*, *Strolers*, and the Like; with the Practice of their Lives, and Manner of Living; which Relation, in itself, is very pleasant, and may serve as a Caution to the Unwary.

Wheedling, What It Is, and How Managed

he Word *Wheedle*, cannot be found to derive itself from any other, and therefore is look'd upon as wholly invented by the *Canters*; but, according as the Sense of it is managed, it signifies a subtle Insinuation into the Humours, Inclinations, Natures and Capacity of any person the *Wheedler* intends to circumvent, or make his Prey; working so effectually, that he possesses them with a Belief, that all his Actions and Services are, as is, indeed, a Kind of Flattery; which, joined with Self-conceit, and the good Opinion we have of ourselves, easily admits of the most favourable Interpretation, since every one is naturally inclined to

Self-love, and thinks his own Abilities in Understanding sufficient, if not the best; it being very observable, that although Men quarrel and contend about Riches and Preferment, one envying another as to those Particulars; none, on the contrary, contend who has the most Wit, or at least grudge not at another's, but conceit their own Stock is sufficient.

> In this they hold that Providence is just,
> And it for Wit, thi' nothing else they trust.

The *Wheedler*'s Business is much in trimming the Sails of Flattery, and forming his Speeches and Actions to the Humour and Constitution of the Person he undertakes, imitating those of whom *Juvenal* the Satyrist makes mention, *viz.* These men, says he, will conform themselves to all sort of Compiny; if you laugh, they will strive to laugh louder; if you are pensive and sad, or prone to weep, they, like Crocodiles, will force feigned Tears; if you complain of Cold, they shiver, as in the Extremity of a Tertian Fit; and if you complain of Heat, even in the Extremity of *December*, they shall puff and pant as if they were in a Manner melted.

> Thus they on Flattery build Foundations bad,
> And only in the empty Air they tread;
> Selling of Wind for Things to support Life,
> And tickle Cullies in their Follies rife.

The Qualifications of the *Wheedler*; and by What Methods and Ways He Works, by Insinuation upon the Passions and Minds of Men, and the Rules be Observes Therein

He or She that sets up for a thriving *Wheedler*, must be no Novice: for if so, there is no apt Qualification for this Science, as they term it, but must first be accommodated with a winning Behaviour, a fluent Tongue, weighty Expression, that can be so cunningly couched, as to make bad seem good, and good bad, to the Eyes and Understanding of the Ignorant; knowing how to time his Management to keep it always in Season: A good Stock of Confidence is likewise required, and a Countenance not subject to a Blush; a Man he must be of infinite jelling, that when he trips, or begins to be discovered in some palpable Flattrey or Dissimulation, he may turn it off, so as either to put a different Construction on the Meaning of his Words, or change his true Meaning into Jest or Ridicule: He must be furnished moreover, with much Patience to bear, without seeming any Way offended, the Impertitence of every Coxcomb or nauseous Fop; and observe his Humours, that he may not be found wanting to tickle the Troat by a seeming Applause and Compliance.

The next Thing he then considers and contemplates, in the Passions of the Mind, and to what they stand most inclined and affected; and this he at first gathers, especially a Hint of them, by the Complexion, Habit and Constitution of the Body; the Complexion attributing to the Sanguine, a merry, jocund Humor, much given to Love and Recreation. To the Melancholy, a morose Temperature of Mind, given to Ease of Body, yet much disturbed at Times in Mind, and prompted by Envy, to undertake malicious Enterprises: To the Flegmatick, he attributes Inconstancy, Sloth, Intemperance, &c. and to the Cholerick, Rashness, and a contentious Disposition, subject to Strife, and Desire of Revenge; and suitable to these, he lays the Line and Plummet of his Flattery or Insinuation, and humours them to his own Advantage in their several Degrees; and, for the most Part, they attack those of the weakest Capacities, with whom they are sure they can be credited, as a cunning Jilt of the Town is made to express herself, *viz.*

You smile to see me, whom the World, per-
     chance,
Mistakes to have some Wit; so far advance
The Int'rests of tame Fools, that I approve
Their Merit more, than Mens of Wit in Love:
But in our Sex too many Proofs there are,
Of those undone by Wits, t'whom Fools repair.
This in my Time was so observ'd a Rule,
Hardly a Wench in Town but had her Fool;
The meanest, common Slut, who long was
     grown
The Jeft and Scorn of every quaint Buffoon,
Had yet left Charms enough to have subdu'd
Some Fop or other, fond to be thought lewd.

Nor is this Art of *Wheedling* altogether unnec-
essary, feeing it carries with it somewhat more
than Wealth; for, by a secret and powerful Charm,
it calms Rage, disarms the threatening Hand of
the Revengeful; moves Compassion in the hard
Hearted, and many Times delivers a Man out of
the Snare. This, and much more, it effects, by a
feigned and flattering Submission, and pretending an untainted and entire Fridneship; whereas,
if there be no downright Enmily, yet there is no
other than the Shadow, or outward Appearance
of a Respect for the Person, to engage him either
to lay aside his present Danger, or perswade and
oblige him to some Kindness extraordinary. But
thus much for this part of *Wheedling*, too much
practised in this Age.

CANT, What It Is, and by Whom It Is Used, with the End to Which It Serves, &c.

ant is found to be the peculiar Language of no Nation; nor is there any Rule prescribed for the Learning or Understanding it, farther than from those who use it to colour over their Villanies, and they are such, for the most part, that call themselves *Egyptians*, but are no other than strolling Beggars, Vagrants, or Wanderers, the Foundation of which Gibberish was laid on one *Rugosa*, a sturdy Wanderer, who first prescribed Rules and Orders for the wandering Tribe, and became their Head, or Superior; but not long enjoyed his ragged Dignity, before he fell sick of a filching

Fever, for which the Doctor of the Triple Tree applied the powerful Cordial of Hemp to his jugular Vein, so that the Strength of the Application not being allay'd in Time, cast him into a dead Sleep, and for ever after spoild his drinking at the Boozing-Ken.

Those that profess this Cant, pretend to be *Egyptians*, hold the People in Hand, especially those that are so foolish as to believe them: That they sucked in the Knowledge of the Stars with their Mother's Milk, and are conversant with the Decrees of Fate, being tee only Kindred of the Destinies, from whom they hide Nothing; nay have so large a Stock of Impudence, as to pretend to Divine Magick, when, indeed, they are no other than a parcel of ignorant, lazy, illiterate Persons, who take up this Kind of Life for the Sake of Bale; yet so much are they feared, as going in great Companies, by the Country People, that they are, in a Manner, forced to give them what they in Reason demand, lest they should fire their Houses, or, as they fondly deem, bewitch their Cattle, when, indeed, the latter is altogether out of their Power; and the greatest Fear that need any Way concern them, is the robbing them of their Pigs, Poultry, Linnen, &c. for which they have divers canting Names or Terms, of which I shall speak hereafter.

The *Canters* have their several Offices and Degrees among them, the Officiators of them being observed and regarded by those that subject themselves as their Inferiors with great Exactness and

Respect; and are distinguished or go under these Denomsnations, viz. The *Upright Man*, who being chosen for his Strength, Archness and Policy, in bringing them off at a dead List, is stiled their Chief, whom all the Rest obey, and among them his Will is a Law during Life, unless he be deposed in a general Assembly or Meeting, which is held twice a Year, in great State, in Places pre-appointed, and most commonly the Suburbs of London, and that for some extraordinary Design; as for the Subversion of their beggarly Commonwealth, &c. and whilst he stands *in statu quo*,[1] all the Morts, Dolls and Doxies, or Women of the several Degrees and Orders among them, are at his Command; as, like wise, the best of whatever they filch or maund, that is, steal or beg.

The *Abram cove*, or *Abraham-man*, is one that dresses himself ridiculously, and pretends, at sundry Times, to be mad, and in Fits, when, indeed, he does it to draw People about him, to procure the Advantage of the Rest, either in telling Fortunes, or giving them the Opportunity of picking the Pockets of the Gazers.

The *Jack man* is their Secretary, who having some small Abilities in Learning, especially in Writing and counterfeiting of Hands, makes it his Business to write their false Passes, false Certificates, and maunding Letters, and is in great Esteem among them.

---

1   Not to be confused with *status quo* (the existing state of affairs), *in statu quo* means in the former or same state. —Ed.

11

The *Dummerers* are such as make a horrible Noise attended with many Antic Postures, and frequently signify not only by Signs, which to every one are not intelligible, but by a forged Writing, that their Tongues were cut out in Turkish Slavery, for reviling the Prophet *Mahomet*, or refusing to comply with his damnable Doctrine; and to that End, and the better to deceive the easy Spectators, and move them to Compassion, they roul back their Tongues, and show as it were only the Root; but if you require to search their Mouth, they will pretend not to underland your Meaning, and with much Clamour refuse it.

The *Patrico* is he that couples them together; the only Ceremony in that kind, consists in placing them with joined Hands over the Carkass of any dead Creature, and bidding them live together till Death parts 'em.

The *Whipjacks* are such as pretend themselves to be Mariners, that have been cast away, and Shipwreck'd either on the Coast, or on some foreign Land, and have nothing to support them in their Travelling to their Habitation: And the better to colour it, pretend a Pass, though it is altogether forged, and they know no more of the Sea than a tame Goose.

The *Fraters* are such as forge Briefs or counterfeit Parents, pretending to beg for decay'd Hospitals, Losses by Fire, and the like; but have been so often detected and punished, that scarce any thing but the Name remains at this Day; for it being a

Public Fraud, 'tis more narrowly pry'd into, than those that are Personal and Private.

The *Paillard* or *Clapperdogeons*, are those that have been brought up to beg from their infancy, and frequently counterfeit Lameness, making their Legs, Arms and Hands appear to be sore, and very nauseous, with Cream and Blood, Butter and Soap, Ointment and Corrosives, and sometimes by putting on counterfeit lame Legs, and false withered Arms, making horrible wry Faces, and setting off their Story of being Shot, Burnt, scalded, perish'd with the Evil, and the like: with a lamentable Voice, and for the most Part they carry Children about with 'em, which they frequently hire of poor Nurses for so much a Week, the better to move Compassion: but if you strictly enquire into their Lameness, you will find it nothing but a Counterfeit of their own devising: and their Sores so flight, that in a Day or two they'd cure of themselves, did they not apply Corrosives.

The *Glimmerers*, are such as go up and down a Maunding, under Pretence they have been undone by Fire, and for the most Part have a forged Certificate with many Names, insinuated to those of the Minister, Justice, and Church-wardens of some remote Parish; pretending great Losses, when indeed their whole Life has been the begging Trade.

The *Mumpers* is the general Beggar, Male and Female, which lie in Cross-Ways, Travel to and fro, carrying for the most Part Children with them, which generally are By-Blows, and delivered to them with a Sum of Money, almost as soon as born.

As for the Women chat attend those stroling Gypsies and Beggars, those that are married after their Fashion, are called *Antem-Morts*; the *Dells* are young Wenches that yet retain their Maidenheads, which by their Custom they must Sacrifice to the *Upright Man*, before they can be free with the Brotherhood.

The *Doxies*, are such as are prostituted to any, and are no other than common Whores of the Kind, among the Brotherhood, and consequently to any Person, if Advantage offers, and for the most Part have the Art of diving into the Pockets of such Cullies they ensnare.

The *Stroling Morts* are such as pretend to be Parsons Widows, or to be born Gentlewomen, and by Marrying against the Consent of their parents, by Losses and Sicknesses are utterly ruined and undone, telling a lamentable Story, to stir up the Minds of the Hearers to compassionate their Sufferings.

The *Baudy-Baskets* are such as wander up and down with a Basket under their Arm, and a Child at their Backs, pretending to sell Toys and Trifles, and so beg or steal as they see Occasion, and find Opportunity.

The *Kitchen Morts* are the little Girls that ran in the Hands of these Gypsies and Beggars, or are carried at their Backs in Blankets.

And these are the chief of the Gang, who from their Head Rendezvous, set out twice a Year, and scatter all over *England*, each Parcel having their appointed Stages, that they may not interfere nor hinder each other, and for that purpose, when they set forward in the Country, they stick up Boughs in the Way of divers kinds, according, as it is agreed among them, that one Company may know which way another is gone, and so take a different Road.

> And so like a Disease they swiftly spread.
> As Locusts muster'd in black Clouds was wed;
> When Egypt felt the Plagues for Pharaoh's Sin,
> And mourn'd the Ruin that it usher'd in.

In What Manner a New-Comer is Received into the Gang of Gypsies and Wandring Beggars, with the Ceremonies That Are Observed, and Other Things

When any Idle Person enters himself into the settled Gang of these Varlets, he is not admitted without Ceremony. And first, being introduced by one of the Gang, the *Upright-Man* demands his Name; which known, he enjoyns him from that Time to renounce it, and to take upon him one familiar to the canting Strain, not understood by the Vulgar: This done, and register'd, his Charge is given him, that he shall be true in all things to the fraternity, and obey to the utmost of his Power, the great Tawny Prince, or, as they style him, the *King of the Gypsies or Strolers*, and keep his

Counsel; that he takes his Part against all that shall oppose him, or any of the Brotherhood, according to the utmost of this ability, not suffering them to be abused by any strange *Pallards, Ruffers, Hookers, Swadlers, Irish Toyls, Dummerers, Jackmen, Whipjacks, Glimmerers, Maunders*, or the like, or any other Outlyers: That he reserve to the Publick Stock the overplus of his gettings: That he will never leave nor forsake the Company of which he has entered a Member, nor teach any, upon what Account soever, the usual Cant proper among them, neither for Favour nor Fear: And lastly, that he will stick close to his *Doxey* or *Rum-Mort*; and then a young Wench is de livered to him as his Mate and Companion by the Patrico, if there be one grown up, if not, he must stay till there is, and be content to be supply'd now and then for Recreation's Sake, by the *Doxies*, who are common among them.

The Adoption being over, the Scouts are commanded abroad, to see if the Coast be clear; and if so, up on the Signal, the Foragers go out and fetch in Crackling Cheats, Grunting Cheats, Margery Praters, Red Shanks, &c. that is, Chickens, Pigs, Hens, and Ducks; some at the same time breaking the Ruffman's Hedges, that is, for firing: Nor does *Tib* of the Buttery, that is, the Geese escape them, while the *Whipjack*, as the most competent Judge, is employed to fetch Rum Booze, or strong Drink from the next Village, with ready Money out of the publick Stock, and if no blind Ale-house out of the Town or Road be near where they use for privateness's Sake to rendezvous, then they make the Fire under a warm Hedge, or in a Gravel-pit, where the Morts are their Cooks; but so slottish in their Dressing, that a Stranger must be wonderfully sharp set, that can find in his Heart to participate of their banquet; and here the old Proverb is truly verify'd, *viz. That the Devil sends Cooks*; yet those that are used to it, feed like Farmers, and account it more Dainty than any other.

The Reasons That Induce Strolers, &c. to Take Up This Kind of Life, and by What Means they Cheat and Deceive the Ignorant Under Pretence of Telling Fortunes

ome may enquire why they delight in this kind of Life; to which I answer, Laziness is the great Motive that induces them to it; and the Gains very considerable, tho' unlawfully gotten: for swarming about the Countries they delude young Wenches that are mad for Husbands, by possessing them they are the Children of the Wise Men, and have familiar Conversation with the Stars, which demonstrate to them future Events; nay, many times they have their Scout or Intelligencer in the Towns and Villages thro' which they are to pass, who against their Arrival enquire out many Things by wheedle or insinuation; as what Things have been lost; who is Sick; who about to be married, or who cross'd in Love, and give Notice thereof privately to the Gypsies, who apply themselves to these Places, with such Protestations of Discovery, and telling none but the Truth, that they get to be believed by repeating what has been told them, with some addition; and that they may seem to conjure, they Cross themselves, and turning up the whites of their Eyes, mutter in an odd Manner their Gibberish; and when they are once found to be in a Truth, the humour of it decoys many to their Lure; and they always have in their Gang some one dextrous at dividing or picking of Pockets; they seldom fail to do it, whilst one of the Crew is poring on the Hand of some silly Wench or Fellow, under Pretence of Fortune-telling; nay, their Children of five or six Years Old, upon the Signal, will do it, which in their gibberish is, *kinching, claw the lower*: which being insensibly performed, occasioned the foolish Report, that if they had one Piece of Money given them, they had the Art of commanding the rest also; indeed in one Sense they have: nor are they wanting if the Cove nap 'm; that is, if they are taxed with it, they make horrid Imprecations that they are Innocent; yet the Whipping-Post is such a powerful Spell attending it, that it many times obliges them to recant their Čant, in making Restitution: Nay, those they carry at their Backs are so dextrous, that they will steal a Hat-Band, loose Head-Cloaths or Handkerchiefs over her Shoulder that carries 'em, whilst she is pretending to tell Fortunes, &c. Nor are those Children for the most Part, any of their own; but when any young Gentlewoman or Servant-Maid has trod awry, and her Reputation and the Father's are to be spar'd, then by the Advice of the Midwife or Nurse, the Child with a Sum of Money, as they can agree, is taken by them; So that these Children but rarely know their true Parents.

Having thus far spoken of the wandring Tribe, who are no other than English Beggars, Thieves and Vagabonds, that discolour their faces, Necks, and Hands with Bacon-Grease and Soot in the Winter, and with green Shell or Husks of Walnuts in the Summer; I shall now proceed to give you an Account of their Cant, and what they mean by it in English.

The *Gypsies'* and *Beggars' CANT*; Comprehending All the Material Words Used by Them, Upon Sundry Occasions; as Likewise Their Explanation

ENGLISH	CANT
 Hand-some Wench	 um-Mort
An Apron	Belly Cheat
A Part or Share	Snack or Earnest
A Break-House	Betty
A Hole	Form
A Gentlewoman	Gentry-Mort
A Receiver of Stoln Goods	Fencing-Cully
A Groat	Flag

A Door	Gige
A Guiny or Job	Husking-Lour
A Child	Kinchen
A little Man	Kinchen-Cove
A private House	Libben
An Alehouse	Boozen-Ken
The Gallows	Nubbing-Cheat
Cloaths	Larries
Thieves	Priggs
Meat or Provision	Peck or Peckeridge
Lace	Peake
A stout Rogue	Ruffer
An Arm	Smiter
Andirons	Glimsenders
To agree with a Man	Famgrasp the Cove
Angry	Glim flushly
A Barboy	Squeaker
A Beadle	Flogging-Cove
Butter	Beaver
Bridwel	Nafkin
Born a Beggar	Clapperdogeon
A Bog-House	Croping-Ken
A Bed	Libbedge
Bread	Penam
Beggers	Maunders
To beg	Maund
A Bottle	Boozing-Cheat
Be careful of what you say	Sto the whids and plant'em

A Bridle	Nabgarder
Shackles	Cramping
A Body	Quarren
Cunning	Queer
Bacon	Ruff Peck
Broker	Fencing-Cully
Bastard	Stalewhimer
Belated	Hoodwink'd
Blind Men	Gropers
A Barn	Skipper
A Bar	Touting-Ken
Be Cautious	Sto the Whids
Broker's Shop	Stolen-Ken
Beaten	Chaft
A Breast	Heaver
A Cheat	Napper
A Coach	Ratler
A Chamber-Pot	Jacum-Gag
A Constable	Hamanbeck
Coach-Beggars	Ratling-Mumpers
A Cloack-Bag	Roger
A Candlestick	Glimstick
Fire	Glimmer
Cut the Cloak-Bag	Flick the Roger
Corn	Grannam
A Cluster of Grapes	Rum boozing Welts
A Crust	Crackler
A Crafty Fellow	Chincher
A Crutch	Lifter

A Church	Autem
To Cheat	Bite
A Sow	Mower
A Coat	Mishtopper
Counterfeit	Confeck
A Coachman	Smacking-Cove
To Copulate	Wap
Cheese	Case
A Cloack	Togeman
The Country	Deausaville
Carriers	Deausaville-Stampers
Shoaked	Frummagem'd
Chickens	Cackling-Cheats
A Dog	Bugher
A Drawer of Wine	Rum Hooper
Day, or Day-Break	Lightmans
Duck	Quacking Cheat
Drunk	Nazzy
A Drunkard	Nazzy-Cove
Drufy	Peeing
Drink	Booze
To enter a House	Dup
Eyes	Ogles or Glaziers
Ends of Gold and Silver	Spangles
Dumb	Cauk
Ditch	Jague
A Drover	Mow-Beater
The Devil	Ruffin
Dry or Thirsty	Chapt

A Ditch	Skew
Fellows that Spirit People	Kidnapers
The Face	Muns
A Fool or Coxcomb	Nizie
Fearful	Peery
To fly or run away	Brush off
One easily over-reached	Cully
Feet	Stampers
Gold	Mint
Coal	Mafkin
Goldsmith	Ridgcully
Gallant	Rum
Garden or Nosegay	Smelling Cheat
To go up Stairs	Track up the Dancert
Glass broken	Filcher snapt
A Highway	Topping Cove
A Highway-Man	Rum-Pad
A Horse-Stealer	Prigger of Prancers
A Horse	Rum-Padder
A Head	Nab
Hat	Nab-Cheat
A Half-Penny	Make
A House	Ken
Hands	Fambles
Hose	Drawers
Hostess	Supouch
Heart	Panter

Host	Buster
To ingage	Blot the Scrip
King of the Link-Boys	Rum-Glimmer
Link Boy	Moon-Curse, or Glim-Jack
Legs	Stampers
Licence	Jacrum
Look thro' the Casement	Tout through the Wicker
Lips	Gans
Lye	Coker
Mass	Solomon
Mallard, or Duck	Redshank or quacking cheat
A Looking glass	Peeper
London	Rumville
Milk-Porridge	Papler
Money	Lower
A Married Woman	Autem-Mort
A Man	Cove
A Nose	Gigg
Newgate	Whit
A Neck	Nub
Night or Evening	Darkman
Pottage	Lap
Pork	Grunting-Cheat
Pease	Thundlers
Partners to Files	Shoulder Shams
A Piece of old Gold	Old Mr. Gory

A Portmanteau	Peter
Any Prison	Quee
A Penny	Win
A Pot or Pipe	Gagg
A Pick-Lock	Gilt
The Plague	Cannakin
Pretty	Dimber
The Pox	Bube
A poor Man	Abraham-Cove
A Purse	Bung
To cut a Purse	Nip the Bung
To speak cunningly	Stow the Whids
To give good Words	Cut the Whids
A Villain	Damber
Rings or Gloves	Pamble-Cheats
A rich Fool	Rum-Cully
Riding	Prigging
Riders	Prigers
A Shilling	Boar or Hog
Sheep	Bleating-Cheats
To steal a Portmanteau	Bite the Roger
A Shirt	Mish
Stockings	Drawers
Stocks	Harmans
Sucking Pigs	Grunting-Cheats
Silver	Witcher
Sixpence	Half a Hog
Silver Bowls	Witcher-Cully

Straw, Sheets, Shoes	Stummel, States, Stamps
A Shop	Swag
Sought for with a Warrant	Romboyl'd
A Sheep-Stealer	Napper of Nayes
A Seal	Jark
Teeth	Crushing-Chats
To lie down	Couch
To go to sleep	Couch a Hodshead
To speak ill	Cut Quere Whids
To be whipp'd	Clay the Jerk
To rob a House	Heave a Booth
Tobacco	Fogus
To take Tobacco	Raise a Cloud
To beat	Fib
To spend or lay out	Fence
To tumble together	Lib
The Sessions-House	Nubbing-Ken
A Turkey	Cobble-Colter
To be transported	Marinated
To run away	Pike off
To look out	Tour
To hang	Trine
The Tongue	Prating-Cheat
To weer	Scour
The Wench has clapt the Fellow	The Mort has tipt the Bubo to the Cully

The Fellow is rubbed off or broken	The Cully is brushed
Make away from the Stars lest you are taken	Blow off the Groundsil
Be judged with hand seal for a Person	Blot the Scrip and jerk
The Rogue was dragged at the Cart's Arse thro' the chief Streets of London, and whipped by the Hangman	The Prancer drew the Quere Cove at the cropping of the rottom through Rumpads of the Rumvill, and was flogg'd by the Nubbing-Cove
Beat the Man on the High-Way, for the Money in his Purse	Fig the Covert quarrons in the Rum-Pad, for the Lour in his Bung
Philip him on the Nose	Give him a rum snatch, or snatchel him on the Gigg
Night-Budge will you spend your Shilling at the next Ale-House	You Dark-man-budge, will you fence your Hog at the next Booze-Ken
Go up Stairs and tip off with the Looking-glass	Track the Dancers and pike with the Peepers

Drawer, fill us presently a Bottle of the best Canary

Rumm hooper, tips presently a Boozing Cheat of Rum-Glutters

Let the Devil take the Justice, and let the Constable hang with his Children about his Neck

The Ruffin nab the Cussinquere, & let the harman-beck trine with his Kinchins about his coloquaron

The Fellow cants very well

The Cully flams Flash rumly

The Fellow entred into Bond with me willingly for forty shillings

The Cully did freely blot the Scrip, and so tipped me forty Hogs

Five Highwaymen got away in the Night out of Newgate

Five Rum-Padders are rubbed in the Darkman out of the Whit

Look thro' the Window and see where the Man walks with Gentlewoman, whose Face is the best I ever saw before

Tout thro' the Wicker and see where the cully pikes with the Gentrymort, whose muns is the rummest I ever touched before

The Drover goes away with the Cows

The Mow-Beater pikes off with the Mows

Cut me some Bread and Cheese

Filsh me some Pannum and case

Host, fill a Pot of Drink	Buffler, fill a Cagg of Rumbooze
Keep your own Ways	Maundo your own pads
Give good Words	Cut been Whids
Give the Money	Tip the Lour
Run for it as well as you can	Pike on the been
Consider well what you say, and lay your Words close	Plant your Whids, and stow them well
The Coach-Beggar has broke the coach-glass	The rattling mumper broke the rattling peeper
The Hue and Cry is belated	The Napping cove is hood-wink'd
The Link-man has robbed the drunken cully of his Purse	The Glimmerer has bit the bubbing cully of his bung
The Horse-Stealer is hanged	The brigger of Prances is nubbed.

Thus, Reader, having given you a Light into this new created Language, which was never known to our Fore-Fathers, nor heard of at the Confusion of *Babel*, I shall proceed to divert you with some pleasant Songs in the same *Lingua*; yet that I may not leave you in the Dark as to the understanding of them, I shall render them likewise into *English*.

Canting *SONGS*; the Best Sort.
In *Cant* and *English*

The Advice, &c.
A Song in Cant.

1. **B**ing out been Morts, rand
   tour and rour
   bing our been Morts, and
   tour and rour
   For all your Duds are bing'd avast,
   the been Cove tips the Lour.
2. I met a Dell, I view'd her well,
   she was been ship to my watch;
   So she and I did stall and cloy
   whatever we could catch.

3. This doxy Dell can cut been whids,
    and wap well for a win,
And drig and cloy so beenishly,
    all the Deauseaville within.

4. The Boyl was up we had good Luck,
    as well in Frost as now;
When they did seek then we did creep,
    and plant in Ruffnan's row.

5. To stroling Ken the Mort brings then,
    to fetch lour for her Cheats;
Duds and Ruffpecks rumboyld by Harmanbecks,
    and won by Maunders feats

6. You Maunders all slow what you stall,
    to Rumcoves that so quier,
And wapping Dell, that niggles well,
    and takes lour for her Hire.

7. And Jybe well jerk, trick some confeck,
    far back by Glimmer to Maund,
To mill each Ken, let Cove bring then,
    through Ruffman's Jaug or Laund,

8. Till cramping's quire, tip Cove his hire,
    and Quire Ken do them catch,
A Canakin will quire Cuffin,
    so quire to been Cove's Watch.

9. Been Darkman's then booze Mort and Ken,
    and been Coves bing avast,
On Chars to trine, by Rum-Cove dine,
    for his long Lib at last,

10. Bing out been Morts, and tout and cour,
    bing out of the Rumvile fine,
A tour the Cove that cloy'd your Duds,

upon the chats to trine.

Now that if any Person should hear one of these
Fellows sing this Song with the Gestures they use
at that time, he would conclude him no better than
a Madman, tho' the *English* or Meaning of it, will
make it more easy and pleasant.

The same Song in English.

1. Go forth, brave Girls: look out, look out,
   look out, I say, good Maids,
For all your Cloaths are stole, I doubt,
   and shar'd amongst the Blades,
2. I met a Lass I lik'd her well,
   with whom I us'd to dally:
What goods we stole, we strait did sell,
   and then abroad did sally.
3. This bouncing Trull can finely talk,
   she will do for a Penny,
Through every Town as she does walk,
   fails not to steal from any.
4. This House being rais'd, aside we slept,
   and through the Mire did wade;
The Hue and Cry, to shun, we crept,
   in Hedges where we lay'd.
5. To the Brokers then my Hedge-Bird flies,
   for Goods she brings good Corn;
Which tho' the Constable after hies,
   our Tricks us away purloins.
6. You maunding Rogues, beware how you

    do steal, for Search is made;
And let each Jade look to it to,
    who will not do till paid.
7. A License got with forged seal,
    to beg as if undone;
By Fire, to break each House and steal,
    o'er Hedge and Ditch to run.
8. Till Shackles soundly pay us Home,
    and to the Goal compel us.
But may some Mischief to 'em come
    who're cruel to good Fellows.
9. Sweet Wench, Alehouse, and Beer, good Night,
    the jovial Rogue's departed,
To hanging by the Justice Spight,
    to his long Home he's carted.
10. Away sweet Ducks with greedy Eyes
    from London walk up Holbourn
Pursue him stole the Cloaths; he flies
    with Hempen Wings to Tyburn.

The King of the GIPSIES *Song,*
made upon his Beloved Doxey or Mistress.

1. Doxy! thy Glaziers fine,
    as Glimmer by the Solomon,
No Gentry Mort hath Parts like thine
    no Cove e'er wap'd with such a one.
2. White thy Fambles, red thy Gan,
    and thy Quarrons dainty is;
Touch a Hogshead with me than,
    and the Darkman's Clip and kiss.

3. What tho' I no Togeman wear,
    nor Commission, Mish, or Slate;
Store of Strammel we'll have here,
    and ith ' Skipper lib in state.
4. Wapping thou I know does love,
    also the Ruffin cly the Mort;
From thy Stamper then remove
    the Drawers, and let us prin in Sport.
5. When the Lightman up does call
    Margery Prater from her Nest,
And her Cackling Cheats withal,
    in a Boozing Ken we'll Feaft.
6. There if Lour we want I'll milk
    a gage or nip from thee a bung;
Rumbooze thou shalt booze thy fill,
    and crash a gruntling Cheats that's young.

In English thus:

1. My bonny Lass, by the Mass I swear,
Thine Eyes doth shine than Fire more clear,
No silken Girl has Thighs like thine,
No Doe more buxom is than mine.
2. Thy Hand is white, and red thy Lip,
Thy dainty Body I will clip;
Let's down to sleep our selves then lay,
Hug in the Dark, and kiss and play.
3. What though I no Cloak do wear,
And neither Shirt nor Sheet do bear,
Yet Straw we'll have enough that's sweet,
And tumble when i'th' Barn we meet.

4. What thy Grandame lov'd doth thou,
Or else you are not kind I vow;
Off then thy with Stockings and Shoes,
And let us do what others use.
5. When the Morning up thall call,
From her Nest the Hen and all,
Her tender Broodings thou and I
Will take and to the Alehouse fly.
6. If we can't our Reckoning pay,
Something I will steal away:
Drink off thy Liquor then thy fill
Some sucking Pig for thee I'll kill.
7. Therefore to London let us hye,
Thou hast a sweet bewitching Eye,
Therefore we'll rob'and kiss Pell-mell,
Escaping Tyburn, all is well.

The Run:-Morts Song,
in Praise of her Maunder,
who had for fakex her.

1. Now my Kinching-Cove is gone,
By the Rum-Pad Maundeth none,
I Qurrons both for Stump and Bone
Like any Clapperdogeon.
2. Dimber damber fare thee well,
Pai-Lards all thou didst excel,
And thy Jockum bore the Bell,
Glimmer on it never fell.
3. Thou the Crange ne'er did scowre,
Harmans had on thee no Power,

Harmanbecks did never tour,
For the Drawers still had lour,
4. Duds and Cheats thou oft has won,
Yet the coffin Quire could shun;
And the Deausaville did'st it run,
Else the Cheats had thee undone,
5. Crank and Dummerar thou couldit play,
Or Run-Maunder in one Day,
And like an Abram-Cove couldit pray,
Yet pass with Gybes well jerk away.
6. When the Darkman's have been wet,
Tho' the Crackman's down didst beat
For Glimmer, whilst a Quacking-Cheat,
Or Rib o'th' Buttery was our Meat.
7. Red-Shanks then I could lack,
Ruff-Peck still hung on my Back,
Crannam ever fill'd my Sack,
With Lap and Poplats held Jack.
8. To thy Bugher and thy Skew,
Filch and Gybes I bid adieu,
Tho the Togeman was not new,
In it the Rogue to me was true.

The Sense in English thus.

1. Now my little Rogue is gone,
By the Highway maudeth none,
In Body both for Strength and Bone,
Like my Clapperdogson.
2. Pretty Rascal fare thee well,
Born Beggars all thou dost excel,

Thy Swipestakes still hall bear the Bell,
No fireship yet abroad it fell,
3. Bolts my Bully ne'er did wear,
Never thou the Stocks did fear;
For thee no Constable did care,
For thou hadst Money and to spare.
4. Cloaths by Stealth thou oft has got,
Yet the Justice took thee not,
But thro' the Country thou didst trot,
The Gallows also had been thy Lot.
5. Dumb and Madman thou could play,
Or a driveling Fool too all the Day,
And the like a poor Man thou coud'st play,
Yet with false Passes 'scape away,
6. When the Evening hath been wet,
For Fire the Hedges down did beat,
We the with stol'n Duck didst treat
Or else a fat Goose was our Meat,
7. Mallards then I could not lack.
Bacon always at my Back,
Nor was Corn wanting in my Sack,
With good Milk-Pottage I held Wrack,
8. To thy Dog and Dish adieu,
The Staff and Pass I ne'er did view,
Tho my Cloak was far from new,
In it my Rogue to me was true.

The Budge's song, in Cant

1. The Budge it is a delicate Trade
   and delicate Trade of Fame,

For when that we have bit the Blow;
    we carry away the Game;
But if the Cully nap us,
    and the Lurries from us take,
O then he rub, us to the Whit,
    though we are not worth a Make,
2. And when that we come to the Whit,
    our Darbies to behold;
And for to do our Pennance there
    we booze the Water cold:
But that when we come out again,
    and the merry Hick we meet,
We file of with his Cole,
    as he pikes along the Street,
3. And when that we have fil'd him,
    perhaps of half a Job;
Then every Man to his Boozing-Ken
    O there to fence his Hog:
But if the Cully nap us,
    and once again we get
Into the Cramping-Rings,
    to scour them in the Whit.
4. Our Fortune soon is told us then,
    unto our Sorrow great,
O we are doom'd by the red Gown-Men,
    to die at the Nubbing-Cheat.
Then every Man with his Mort in his Hand,
    does booze off his Cag, and Part,
With a Kiss we part, and Westward stand
    to the Nubbinug-Cheat in a Cart.
5. And when we come to the Nubbing-Cheat,

for rubbing on the Budge;
There stands Jack Ketch, that Son of a Bitch,
    that owes us all a Grudge:
For when that he has nubb'd us,
    and our Friends tip him no Cole,
He takes his Chive and cut us down,
    and tips us into a Hole.

Besides the stroling Beggars and pretended Egyptians, there are others that use the Cant, who are most of the Town Thieves; or such as harbour about London, and are distinguished by several canting Names and Titles, *viz.*

The High-Pad, or Highway-Man. The Low-Pad, or Foot-Robber. The Budge, who makes it his business to run into Houses, and take what comes first to hand. The Diver, Pick-Pocket. The Bulk, or one that is his Assistant, in creating Quarrels by jostling, &c. to gather a Crowd that the Divermay have a better Opportunity to effect his purpose. The Jilt is one that pretending Business in a Tavern or Alehouse, takes a private Room, and with Pick-Locks opens the Trunks or Chests, and taking what he can conveniently, looks 'em again, pays his Reckoning and departs. The Prigger of Prancers is one that makes it his Bugness to steal Horses. The Ken-Miller is one that robs Houses in the Night-Time, by breaking them open, or getting in at the Window, and seldom goes alone. The File is the same with the Diver, tho' for the most part he goes without the Bulk, and was formerly known by the Title of the Bung-Nipper, because with a horn Thumb and sharp Knife, he used to cut the Pockets clear off, with all that was in them. The Shop-Lifts are commonly Women, who go into Shops under pretence of Buying, and seeming very difficult to be pleas'd, find an opportunity to flip some Garments, Piece of Silk or Stuff, &c. into the Coat, Bag, or other private Conveyance, with which they are seldom unfurnished. The Angler is one that takes a Quarry of Glass out of a Casement, and so opening it, with a long Pole and Hook at the End on't, pulls to him what he can conveniently reach, without entring the House. But enough of these Varlets that like the Egyptian Locusts pester the Nation, there being no Remedy effectual to put an End to their Rogueries but the Gallows; wherefore not to trouble the Reader with a Story of their many Villainies, and by what Means they atchieve them, all of them being witty and ingenious in Mischief; I shall conclude this Discourse with a Song very suitable to the Purpose.

The black Profession: A SONG

GOOD People give Ear, whist a Story I tell
Of twenty black Tradesmen who were
    brought up in Hell,
On purpose poor People to rob of their Due,
There's none shall be nooz'd if you find but
    one true.
The First was a Coiner that stampt in a Mold,

The Second a Voucher to put of his Gold:
> *Mark you well, heark well,*
> *See where they're rubb'd*
> *Up to the Nubbing-Cheat, and there*
> *they're nubb'd.*

The Third was a Padder that fell to decay,
And when he was living, took to the High-Way
The Fourth is a Milken, to crack up a Door,
He'll venture to rob both the Rich and Poor
The Fifth is a Glazier, who when he creeps in,
To pinch all the Lurry he thinks it no Sin:
> *Mark you,well,&c.*

The Sixth is a File-Coy that not one Hick spares,
The Seventh is a Budge, to trip up the Stairs.
The Eighth is a Bulk that can bulk and hick,
If ihe Master be napp'd, then the Bulk he is sick.
The Ninth is a Ginny, to lift up the Grate,
If he sees but the Lurry with his Hooks he will bait.
> *Mark you well, &c.*

The Tenth it is a Shop-Lift, who carries a Bob,
When the rangeth the City the Shops for to rob.
The Eleventh is a Bubber, much used of late,
He goes to an Alehouse and steals thence a Plate.
The Twelfth a Trapan, if a Cully he does meet,
He nips all his Lour and turns him i'th Street.
> *Mark you well, & c.*

The Thirteenth a Fambler false Rings for to sell,
When a Mob he has bit, his Cole he will tell.
The Fourteenth a Gamester, if he sees the
> Hick sweet,
He presently drops down a Cog in the Street,

The Fifteenth a Prancer whose Courage is small,
If they catch him Horse stealing he's nooz'd for all.
    Mark you well, & c.
The Sixteenth a Sheep-napper, whose Trade
    is so deep,
If he's caught in the Corn he's mark'd for a Sheep.
The Seventeeth a Dunakar that will make Vows
To go into the Country to steal all the Cows.
The Eighteenth a Kid-Napper, who spirits
    young Men,
Tho he tips them the Pikes they nig him again:
    Mark you well, & c.
The Nineteeth is a Prigger of Canklets in Storms,
Goes to the Country to visit the Farms,
He steals there the Poultry, and thinks it no Sin,
When in the Henrooft i'th' Night he gets in.
The Twentieth a Thief-Taker, so we him call,
If he haps a poor Tradesman he makes him pay all.

A S O N G

There is a black and fullen Hour,
    Which Fate decreed our Life shou'd know;
Left we should flight Almighty Pow'r,
    Rapt with the Joys we find below:
'Tis past, dear Cynthia! now let Frowns be gone,
    For Crimes alas! to me unknown.

In such soft Hour of silent Night,
    your Image in a Dream appears;
I grasp the Soul of my Delight,

slumber in Joy, but wake in Tears
Ah! faithless charming, Saint, what will you do?
Let me not think I am by you,
   lov'd worse, lov'd worse, for being true.

We do not mean, by this Publication, to offer any Injury to those whom the Frowns of Fortune have rendered miserable and proper Objects of Compasion: No—those poor Creatures we pity, and would gladly relieve. The Design and Business of this Pamphlet therefore is to fix such a mark upon the Wicked, that the artful Deceivers may be known from those who are in real Distress; in order that the one may be brought to Justice, and the other pointed out as pro per Objects for the Alms of the charitable and well disposed Christian, who will, I hope, always consider, that by giving to the Poor they lend unto the Lord.

F I N I S